W9-CEB-229

THE AZTEC CIVILIZATION

MOMENTS IN HISTORY

BY SHIRLEY JORDAN

Perfection Learning®

ABOUT THE AUTHOR

Shirley Jordan is a retired elementary school teacher and principal. She is currently a lecturer in the teacher-training program at California State University, Fullerton, California.

Shirley loves to travel—with a preference for sites important to U.S. history. She has had more than 50 travel articles published in recent years. It was through her travels that she became interested in "moments in history," those ironic and little-known stories that make one exclaim, "I didn't know that!" Such stories are woven throughout her books.

Text © 2001 by **Perfection Learning® Corporation**.
Printed in the United States of America. For information, contact

Perfection Learning® Corporation
1000 North Second Avenue, P.O. Box 500
Logan, Iowa 51546-0500.
Tel: 1-800-831-4190 • Fax: 1-712-644-2392
perfectionlearning.com

Paperback ISBN 0-7891-5497-8
Cover Craft® ISBN 0-7569-0246-0

5 6 7 8 9 SP 10 09 08 07 06

TABLE OF CONTENTS

The ruins of the Templo Mayor in modern-day Mexico City, which was founded on the site of Tenochtitlán.

A Timeline of Important Events

1168 A.D.	The Aztecs, a small tribe of hunters and gatherers, leave their home in northern Mexico. They wander south, looking for new land. They settle in several places. But they move on after a year or two.
1323	The Aztecs find a rocky island in a marshy lake called Texcoco. They see the sign they have been waiting for. It is an eagle with a snake in its beak, sitting on a cactus.
1427	After years of paying taxes called **tribute** to other tribal leaders, the Aztecs join people of three other towns to rise up against their rulers. Itzcóatl (eets-KO-atl) is the chief who leads them in this revolt.
1427–1440	Under Itzcóatl, the Aztecs conquer 24 towns.
1440–1469	Montezuma I comes to power. His army conquers other valley peoples. His builders construct a long **dike** to hold back Lake Texcoco and enlarge the city.

1469–1479	Axayacatl, the son of Montezuma I, becomes chief of the Aztecs. He conquers many rich cities. Now the Aztec empire reaches to the Pacific Ocean.
1479–1486	Tizoc, another son of Montezuma I, comes to the throne. He founds the Great Temple. Calling him a coward, his own military leaders poison him.
1486–1503	Under Tizoc's brother, Ahuitzotl, the Aztec warriors continue to move into other cities. The empire now spreads south to Guatemala and east to the Gulf of Mexico.
1503–1520	Montezuma II, a nephew of Ahuitzotl, becomes the last great ruler of the Aztecs. His warriors conquer many enemies. Now, 400 towns are paying tributes to Montezuma II.
1519	Montezuma II learns that Spanish forces, under Hernán Cortés, have landed at Vera Cruz. They are marching toward his capital, Tenochtitlán. Later, Montezuma II dies while being held prisoner by the Spanish.
1521	After a long battle, the Spanish conquest of the Aztecs is complete.
1535	All of Mexico becomes a colony of Spain.

Excavation of Great Temple stairs in Mexico City

5

This picture record shows how the Aztecs founded Tenochtitlán. The border symbols show the years in the Aztec calendar.

THE AZTEC PEOPLE FIND A HOME

Hundreds of years ago, the ancestors of the Aztec people lived in northern Mexico. They did not yet know about the broad, rich valley where Mexico City now stands.

These early Aztecs were hunters and gatherers. But in their wanderings, they had never found a place to settle. For more than 150 years, no spot seemed quite right. Children were born, grew up, had children of their own, and died. Still the Aztecs wandered from place to place without a homeland.

About 1300 A.D., legend tells of a message received by the Aztecs. It came from a god they worshiped called Huitzilopochtli (wee-tseel-o-POTCH-tlee), or Blue Hummingbird. This god told the Aztec priests that the wandering families should go south, into the Valley of Mexico. At the right spot, they would find an eagle sitting on a cactus. The eagle would have a snake in its mouth.

Happy to have a message, the Aztecs made their way toward the Valley of Mexico.

But the valley had already been home to settlers. An early tribe, the Olmecs, had first farmed the rich soil. When the Olmecs lost power, another southern tribe, the Zapotecs, had taken their place.

But the Zapotecs were not strong enough to keep their power over the valley.

Serpent heads on Olmec ruins, Teotihuacan (below)

8

The Toltecs, a fierce tribe, soon came and forced them off the land.

The Toltecs were not just good at fighting. They were skilled workers too. They built the fine city of Tula. Master builders made huge monuments cut from stone. Toltec crafts and artwork were highly advanced.

The Toltec farmers did their jobs well too. Some years, the crops grew taller than a human.

Toltec mural, Tula (below)

9

Toltec warrior roof supports, Tula

But gifted as they were, the Toltecs were also a savage race. They carved idols of demon gods. And they believed human sacrifices would please the many gods they worshiped. Almost every day, they killed an enemy prisoner to honor one god or another.

Around the year 1168, the proud city of Tula was attacked and destroyed by other fierce tribes. The Toltecs were defeated and driven away from their valley. Their streets stood empty. Sometimes wandering **barbarians** roamed the city and camped there for a time.

More than 100 years passed. The wandering Aztecs were settling farther and farther south. They were coming close to the Valley of Mexico, the former land of the Toltecs. Whenever they stopped to settle in a new place, they looked for the sign Blue Hummingbird had promised.

Finally, in 1323, the Aztecs arrived at an island in the marshy Valley of Mexico. All around them was a shallow, salty lake. They named it Texcoco. And here they found the sign they had been searching for—an eagle with a snake in its beak, sitting on a cactus.

They named this place Tenochtitlán (te-notch-ti-TLAHN), which meant "place of the prickly pear cactus." They built a temple to Blue Hummingbird. Then they fashioned huts around the temple from reeds.

MEXICO.

At first, there was no food. Crops for harvest required a full planting season. And it was too late now. So the new settlers were forced to eat fish, frogs, and waterbirds.

Blue Hummingbird had led the Aztecs to a fine place. But they did not have their independence.

A nearby tribe, the Tepanecs, sent warriors to force the Aztecs to pay their finest possessions as tribute to the Tepanec king. Also, the Aztec men were forced to fight as soldiers for that king.

These unhappy conditions lasted about 100 years. Then the Aztecs joined three other groups who were also paying tribute.

Under a warrior leader, Itzcóatl, the towns revolted against their captors. Soon they won their independence. Excited by their victory, Itzcóatl and his people decided to conquer other parts of the valley.

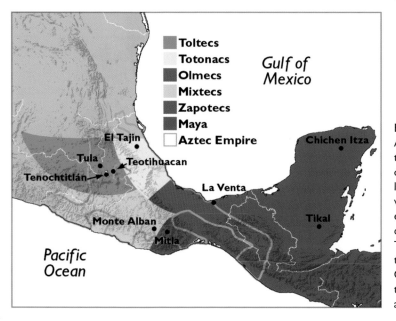

Toltecs
Totonacs
Olmecs
Mixtecs
Zapotecs
Maya
Aztec Empire

Gulf of Mexico

El Tajin
Tula
Teotihuacan
Tenochtitlán
La Venta
Monte Alban
Mitla
Chichen Itza
Tikal

Pacific Ocean

Before the Aztecs began their empire, other peoples lived in what would eventually be called Mexico. The first of these, the Olmecs, began their civilization about 1300 B.C.

As years passed, the Aztecs won battles. They took over more and more land until they had settled the whole valley. Now others were paying tribute to *them*. Through their wars, they grew richer and richer from the treasures of those they had conquered. Each year, the warriors marched out of the valley to conquer lands to the east and the west.

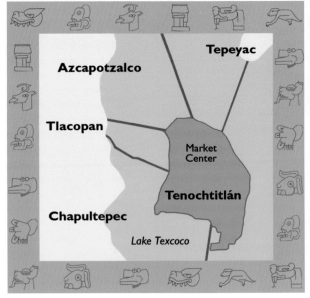

In less than 100 years, the Aztecs became masters of an empire. It stretched from the Pacific Ocean to the Gulf of Mexico. By 1519, about 500 towns and 15 million people lived under the rule of this empire.

It seemed as if nothing could ever bring it down.

THE AZTECS AND THEIR GODS

Religion was important to the Aztecs. The people believed in many gods. Each one was important to a certain part of a family's life.

Farmers sought help from gods who ruled the sun and the rain. Artists and traders worshiped gods they believed brought them good or bad fortune.

All together, the Aztecs had hundreds of such gods. To honor them, the people held many religious ceremonies.

As the Aztec empire grew larger, neighboring tribes brought stories about their gods. Many were adopted by the Aztecs. These gods were added to those they already believed in.

The Aztec priests taught that the earth was a flat, round disk. It was surrounded by water. Each direction from this disk had a different heaven. The soul of a brave warrior who had died went east to the heaven of the sun. Souls of women who had died when their children were born went to a paradise in the west.

Aztec priests

Everyone else traveled to the north. There their souls were ruled by the Lord and Lady of Death. They were in charge of the hell on that side of the earth. These two are often shown in Aztec paintings. They wear masks made from human skulls.

Three Important Aztec Gods

QUETZALCÓATL

Quetzalcóatl (kayt-zahl-KO-atl) appears in hundreds of paintings and statues. He wore a mask like a bird's beak. And he had a bearded chin.

The Aztecs worshiped this god as their Feathered Serpent. He was the peace-loving god of learning and the priesthood. In paintings, he is always shown with a *quetzal*, a bird much like a pheasant. The feathers of the quetzal were considered sacred and could be worn only by important nobles or the king.

So loved was this god that he was thought to have many roles. He was the god of life, wind, creation, and twins. The Aztecs believed he taught people how to plant, work with metal, and construct beautiful buildings.

The most unusual thing about Quetzalcóatl was that paintings always showed him with light-colored skin. Legend said he had been a leader of the ancient Toltec people.

The worship of Quetzalcóatl as a white god would later lead the Aztec civilization to grave danger when fair-skinned men arrived from across the sea.

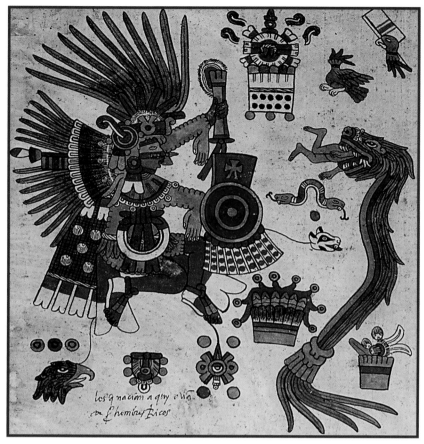

Tezcatlipoca, "Smoking Mirror," (left) and Quetzalcóatl, "Feathered Serpent" (right)

TEZCATLIPOCA

Tezcatlipoca (tes-kaht-lee-PO-ka) was the god of night. He was also considered the chief of the gods. His name meant "Smoking Mirror." The Aztecs believed he could see everything on earth in a mirror attached to his right foot. He was the god of *sorcery*, or magic. And he was also known as the god of darkness.

This god had a special role in the legend of Quetzalcóatl. The ancient Toltec peoples had believed Quetzalcóatl was a human leader as well as a god. According to their legend, Tezcatlipoca had driven Quetzalcóatl away from his people.

Quetzalcóatl wandered for a long time. Then he disappeared across the eastern sea. But before he left, he promised to return in the year *ce acatl,* which means "one reed." This special year on the Aztec calendar came around only every 52 years.

The people believed in the Toltec legend of Quetzalcóatl. They waited for his return.

HUITZILOPOCHTLI

The god of war, hunting, and the noonday sun was Huitzilopochtli. About 1300 A.D., in his earlier role as the god Blue Hummingbird, he had told the Aztec people to

The goddess Coatlicue, mother of Huitzilopochtli

travel to their new land and find the eagle standing on a cactus with a snake in its mouth.

As god of war, Huitzilopochtli was the giver of victory in battle. He was also the special god of young warriors. Aztec boys began this training when they were eight years old.

On the great pyramid in the city of Tenochtitlán, a shrine stood to this powerful god. He was shown as a short, squatty stone figure, covered with gold. Nestled into the gold were precious stones and dozens of pearls.

Around his waist was a belt. It was made in the form of large snakes, coiled around one another. These were fashioned in gold and decorated with more precious stones. A necklace of gold masks and silver hearts hung around his neck.

A great snakeskin drum on the temple sounded nine times each day. Its tones marked ceremonies to honor Huitzilopochtli, who demanded large numbers of human sacrifices. The people believed this cruel and frightening god insisted upon the sacrifice of beating hearts, freshly torn from their victims.

The image shows an Aztec codex illustration with handwritten Spanish annotations including "la partera", "las ynsignias", "cuna con criatura", and other text.

The first days in a baby's life. After babies were born, they were told that they had to work hard throughout their lives. On the left, a mother talks to her newborn baby. The four symbols above the baby show that this child is four days old. On a special day chosen by the priest, the baby was bathed and named, as shown on the right.

CHAPTER 3

THE AZTEC FAMILY

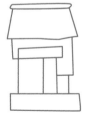

When an Aztec wife had a baby, another woman called a *midwife* helped her bring the child into the world. And right from the very first moments of the baby's life, the midwife spoke to the child. If the baby was a boy, the midwife told him he would be a great warrior. If it was a girl, she told the small baby she must stay at home and look after her family.

Other family members from the village came to see the new baby. They gave more good advice. The Aztecs loved their children very much. They wanted their babies to know all about the world they had been born into.

17

The very day their child was born, parents consulted with a priest. This was very important. They believed some days were lucky and some days were unlucky. Only the priest could tell what kind of day it was. He looked into his special "book of fate" to find out.

If the book of fate said the birth date was unlucky, the child would not be named until the priest found a day with a better fortune. But if the real day of the birth was a lucky one, the child was scheduled to be named in a ceremony to take place four days later.

The date of birth was important. The Aztecs believed a person's character was set by that date. For instance, Rabbit was the sign of drunkenness. So a child born under the sign of Rabbit would end up a drunk.

After the naming day was set, four young boys were invited to the house. The midwife set the baby down on a mat near the boys. If the baby was a boy, she put small copies of his father's tools next to him. On his other side, she placed a warrior's shield. These would guide him toward future work pleasing to the gods.

If the newborn child was a girl, the midwife gave her a small workbasket and a spindle for making thread. She showed the child how to use them. Then she took a broom and told the baby what it was. As the child lay on the mat, the midwife swept the room. She showed the baby how the task should be done.

After these things were done, the four young boys who had watched the ceremony ran through the village. There they hurried back and forth, telling everyone the new baby's name. Relatives and friends gathered and feasted to express their joy.

At the age of three, more training began for Aztec children. Part of that training concerned the food the children would be allowed to eat.

Aztec children did not just eat until they were full. And they did not eat whenever they wanted.

Three-year-olds were allowed only one-half of a corn cake

Five- and six-year-olds are taught by their parents. Blue dots indicate the ages of the children, and the yellow shapes show how many corn cakes children were given to eat each day. Boys (left) helped their fathers by carrying loads, while girls (right) learned to spin.

each day, along with vegetables and fish. When children reached age 4, they received a full corn cake. And between the ages of 6 and 12, they were given a corn cake and a half. Only when children were 13 or older could they have two corn cakes with their other foods.

These rules were not set down because food was scarce. The Aztecs believed withholding food taught discipline.

Parents trained their young children to help with simple tasks around the house. A favorite job for boys three and up was to shoo the birds and animals away from the family's crops.

By the age of six, an Aztec boy began to learn how to farm and catch fish. He would need to know how to build a fire and handle a canoe. All these things he learned from his father.

While a boy was learning these things, his mother taught his sisters to spin thread, weave cloth, and sew. She showed her daughters how to cook meat and fish and how to grind the corn for corn cakes.

19

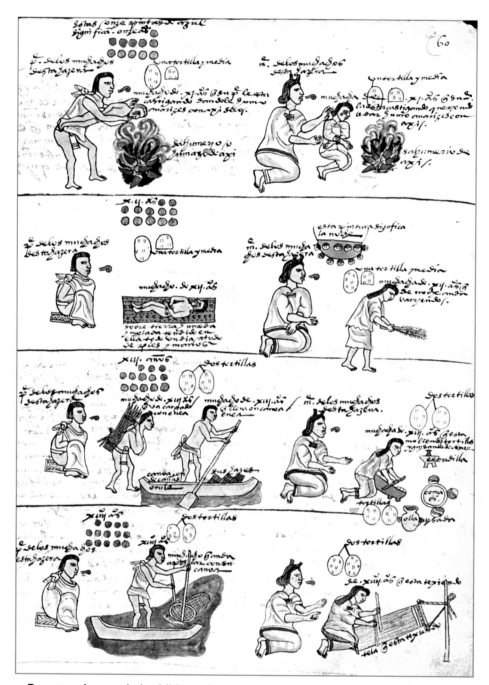

Parents educate their children. On the top row, eleven-year-olds are held over burning hot peppers. Twelve-year-olds in the second row listen to a lecture and learn to sweep. Thirteen-year-olds in the third row carry goods and learn to cook. The bottom row shows fourteen-year-olds learning to fish and weave. Yellow shapes above each picture show how many corn cakes children were given to eat each day.

Aztec children were watched very closely by their parents. They did not often misbehave. When they did, their punishment was strict. A parent might prick the hand of a disobeying child with a needle from the *maguey* plant. The prick would make the hand bleed.

For another punishment, a child might be tied up all day or all night. The child would stand on wet earth or in a shallow pond.

But the punishment children feared the most involved hot peppers grown in the Aztec fields. The parents gathered a large pile of peppers. Then they burned the peppers in an open fire. Naughty children were forced to lean over the smoke coming from the fire. The burning peppers would make the children's eyes water and sting until they were in great pain.

The maguey cactus grew wild in the Valley of Mexico. The Aztecs used its thorns for needles. Its fiber became their rope and could be woven into cloth. The plant's sap, when allowed to **ferment**, became a powerful liquor called *pulque*.

Schooling was important in Aztec life. Parents sent their children to separate schools at the age of seven. *Telpochcalli*, or House of Youth, were schools for the sons of the peasants. And *calmecac* schools were for the sons of nobles.

The students in the telpochcalli school learned religion, **humility**, and obedience. They also learned to use weapons to protect their city. The food was plain, and there was not a large amount of it.

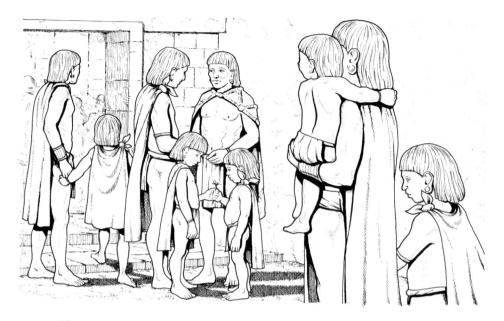

The calmecac school was run by the priests. Even if a young boy was to become a priest later, he had to work hard and give up many favorite foods. He had to learn everything taught in the telpochcalli school. He would have to know mathematics, astronomy, law, and writing. And he would be expected to be a hero in battle.

Girls from noble families could also attend calmecac. Here they trained to be priestesses or wives of important officials.

The schools for girls were taught by priestesses. Here they learned how to wear makeup. Yellow skin was thought to be especially beautiful. So the girls painted their skins with a yellow cream made from crushed beetles. Girls also rubbed black mud into their short hair. Then they dyed it blue with the indigo plant. They dyed their teeth bright red with thousands of tiny, crushed insects called *cochineals*. On their hands and necks, they painted symbols of favorite gods.

Such were the signs of beauty in the Aztec world.

Cochineals on a prickly pear cactus

CHAPTER 4

LIFE AMONG THE COMMON PEOPLE

Even though their empire was wealthy, not every Aztec was a rich person.

Only a noble owned his own land. Among the commoners, land ownership was held by the *calpulli,* a council of blood-related family members. The calpulli met each year to divide the land by household. They did this because some sons had married, and some of the oldest family members had died.

Sometimes a member of the family was found to have been lazy in caring for the fields. Crops had weakened and died. That person's land was quickly taken away. This meant the unfortunate person would have to work as a slave for a noble in order to eat.

The average family farm was about ten acres in size. But only a portion of that land could be planted at one time. For two years, the fine, black soil would produce corn, beans, sweet potatoes, peppers, and squashes. There was more than a family could eat. This allowed the people to trade their extra crops to pay taxes or buy clothing, meat, or weapons.

But after two years, the land lost its fertile qualities. So the soil had to rest. It would lie *fallow,* or unused, for ten years.

Because Tenochtitlán had been built upon a few small islands in the middle of a lake, the Aztecs needed a way to make more land for farming.

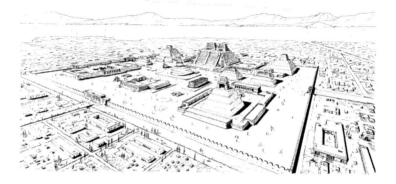

Let's meet Tomac, a young Aztec boy. He is learning how to **reclaim** *land from the lake.*

The pounding of the drum on top of the temple and the eerie wail of the **conch** shell awaken 13-year-old Tomac. It is dark outside. But he knows it is time to get up. The drum and conch will sound eight more times during the day. The next sounding will be at dawn. Tomac and his father must be on their way by then. They will pole their flat-bottomed boat through the **canals** and across the waters of the lake.

Tomac hears his mother moving about inside their mud hut. She builds a small, low fire. It must not flame too high. The roof is made of reeds from the lake and **thatch** from the maguey plant. These materials burn easily. So it is important to keep the fire low and watch it carefully.

Mother has boiled corn and is grinding it in the hollowed-out slab of stone called a *metate.* Soon large, flat round cakes will be cooking on a clay cooking plate called a *comalli.*

Some mornings, Tomac and his father leave without eating. But today, the corn cakes smell especially good. Tomac must hurry if there is to be time for some.

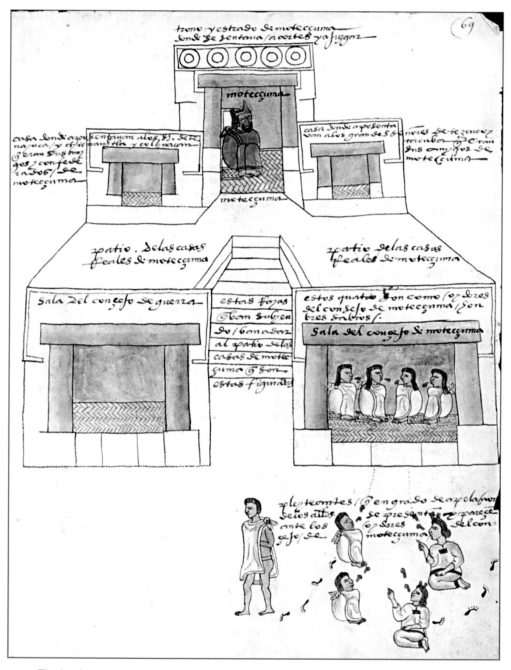

The king's palace had a main building with older buildings around it. The second floor of the main palace housed the king (shown in blue above). Offices and storerooms were on the first floor. There were gardens and courtyards among the buildings. Walls were painted with colorful decorations.

Because the Aztecs loved bright colors, the patios and flat roofs of the city's most important buildings were covered with flowering plants. Red, green, yellow, and purple blossoms spilled over the walls, splashing color against the white background.

Inside the king's palace or a noble's house, the rooms were almost bare except for mats for sleeping. Wooden torches attached to the walls were the source of light in the evening. There were no doors that would close. In any opening to the outside hung a wide cloth decorated with copper bells. This simple plan allowed cool air to pass through the house. This cooled the inside air and added a cheerful sound.

The Aztecs liked to be clean. Most noble families had a bathhouse in the garden. It was built of mud and brick. Servants lit a fire against the back wall. Then a member of the noble family crawled into the bathhouse. Then the servants threw water against the hot inside wall. The bath chamber filled with steam.

With the steam all around him, the bather beat himself with sticks to make his skin clean. If a man was not rich enough to have a bathhouse, he still wanted to be clean. So he would bathe in the lake each day.

Noble families loved to wear bright colors. They dressed in bright feathers, dyed and **embroidered** cloaks, and dramatic headdresses. They carried fans and flowers. When a feast or dance was coming, the young nobles dyed their bodies black, a color they believed made them look handsome.

The Aztecs loved art and music. In addition to the bright colors they favored, they admired the metal work crafted by their **artisans**. So they wore a great deal of jewelry. The best of the jewelry makers were descended from an earlier tribe in the valley, the Toltecs. Because of this, the Aztecs used the word *tolteca* to mean "an artist who forms fine articles with his hands."

Parties were a special treat for the rich and important citizens. For days, slaves would cook the meat of deer and rabbits brought back by hunters. Or there might be turkeys and dogs that had been raised on the palace grounds.

Guests came in their finest clothes and often brought brightly colored flowers to their hosts. Soon the home was overflowing with color and pleasant smells.

Music was very popular with the noble families. Many of the more wealthy households had their own orchestras of drums and rattles. The flute was a special favorite of the Aztecs. It was the only instrument they had that carried a melody.

After feasting on favorite foods, the party guests settled back to enjoy a favorite cocoa drink. Jugglers and dancers entertained for hours.

Most parties lasted all night. The next day, while the hosts slept, their slaves cleaned the house and put everything back in order.

CHAPTER 6

THE ARTISANS AND THE MERCHANTS

There were two groups of Aztecs who were neither nobles nor common people. They had special roles in the Aztec kingdom.

The Artisans

These craftsmen lived in a separate part of the city. If they came from another tribe, they might worship their own gods. And instead of sending their sons to the calmecac or telpochcalli schools, they trained them in the skills needed to someday take their place.

At first, a sculptor might give his son some sand and show him how to polish a finished piece. After the child learned that job, the sculptor might give the boy a copper knife and teach him to help carve a shape in jade, crystal, or **obsidian**.

A goldsmith would show his son how to make a model in clay, cover it with beeswax, and cover it again with clay.

When the clay hardened, he would remove the model. Then he would pour in molten gold and let it cool. When he broke open the mold, the shape was revealed.

Feather working was a craft both boys and girls might learn. First the artisan made a design on a piece of cloth glued to cactus stalks. Then the whole family gathered feathers from the many birds of the area. Using a sticky substance made from bat droppings, the artist stuck the feathers onto the cloth. Soon the feather painting looked like the design.

The most elegant feathers came from the green quetzal bird and the rare turquoise hummingbird. Only the richest families could afford a piece of featherwork with these.

The Merchants

This second group of Aztecs trained their sons to take over their jobs.

The merchants spent all their time trading. And to do this, they traveled long distances. They might be gone from home for months at a time.

A merchant might go north to obtain blue turquoise from the Pueblo Indians. He might go east to trade with the Maya for cocoa beans. To the south, tribes had parrot feathers to **barter**. And to the west lay gold and silver. For protection from wandering thieves, wise merchants traveled in large groups.

When they were not away on a trading journey, the merchants lived in their own area of the city. Here they pretended to be poor. They wore plain clothing and kept to themselves. They hoped this would fool thieves that might be watching them.

To help convince others they were poor, merchants often returned to the city quietly. They entered through the city's back gate after dark. This way, no one else knew what treasures they might be carrying.

CHAPTER 7

TRAINING A YOUNG PRIEST

The brightest of the Aztec children were chosen to go to the calmecac school. This was a great honor for a family.

Let us meet Sonan, a boy who has just reached his eighth birthday.

This is an exciting day for Sonan. He is to begin his training as an Aztec priest.

When he wakes up in the morning, he first says his prayers to Quetzalcóatl, the god of priests. Sonan hopes he can learn all the things he must know for his important job. He knows that girls are sometimes trained to be priests too. He knows his younger sister will want to be chosen someday.

As soon as he arrives at the school, Sonan can tell that the new life will not be easy. The morning is spent learning to read and write the Aztec language. By the end of the morning, Sonan is very tired and hungry.

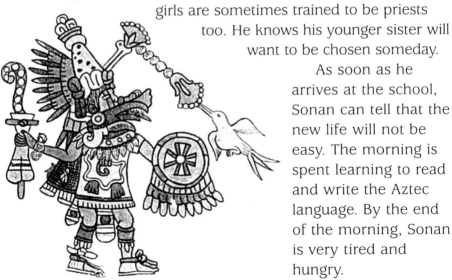

Quetzalcóatl

But what is this? The midday meal for the boys and girls in training is a tortilla and some water. The tortilla tastes like the corn cakes Sonan's mother makes. But it is flatter. And it has no filling. He thinks of the fruits, beans, squash, or tomatoes his mother would have added to his meal. And at home, he would have been allowed a tortilla and a half.

Just as he is thinking about how hungry he is, another boy whispers that sometimes the student priests **fast** for one or more days. During those times, they don't eat at all.

When night comes, the boys and girls sleep on the bare floor. Sonan is used to having the floor for his bed, but he has always had a woven mat under him.

He does not sleep very well the first night. But perhaps that is a good thing. Two times each night, the boys and girls must get up to pray. After the second time, they are sent outside to the edge of the lake. There they must gather black beetles. Later, they squeeze liquid from the insects. This liquid will become the black body paint priests cover themselves with.

In the morning, the boys and girls line up to sacrifice blood. This will please the gods. Sonan is handed a long, sharp thorn. He must prick his tongue and let the blood drip. All the other students do the same.

Each day, a *quail*, a large bird like a fat pigeon, is brought to the calmecac priests. It is to be sacrificed. Its beating heart is the daily offering to the sun god.

As the days and years pass, Sonan continues his studies. By now, he is used to the harsh life. He no longer wonders why his

stomach can never be full. He knows why. A priest must learn discipline.

He reads and writes with great skill now. He has studied the sun, moon, and stars. He knows the heavens and when an **eclipse** will happen. He can read the sacred calendar and learn the lucky and unlucky days. He has learned to judge the coming of a drought. He can find the signs that tell of approaching famine.

A different god controls each period of 13 days. These periods repeat 20 times in a year. This makes the 260-day sacred calendar. It is a way of marking time that the Aztecs have borrowed from the Maya to the east of them.

Sonan knows about all the gods his people worship. He knows the prayers that make the gods happy. And he sings the tunes that please them.

As Sonan grows older, he must make a decision. Priests may not marry. So when Sonan is 20, he must decide whether he will continue as a priest.

Calendar making

37

Some of his friends have decided to leave the priesthood to marry and raise families. They will use their skills from the calmecac school to become doctors or fortune-tellers. And because they can read and write, many will become **scribes**.

When his twentieth birthday arrives, Sonan decides to continue in the life of a priest. He will become a messenger of the gods. From now on, his duties will be at the temple.

A huge square in the middle of the city is the Temple Precinct. Each side stretches for more than 300 **meters**, longer than three soccer fields. Around the edges of the Temple Precinct is a huge wall called the Serpent Wall. It is carved to look like giant rattlesnakes.

Stone serpent located near Templo Mayor

Two huge towering temples rise in the middle of the Temple Precinct. One is blue. It is dedicated to Tlaloc, the god of rain and good crops. Next to it stands the mighty

temple of the war god, Huitzilopochtli, giver of victory to brave warriors. Each temple has a long staircase that leads to an altar for sacrifices.

The day comes when the young priest Sonan, covered with black body paint, will claim his first sacrifice. Arriving at the temple, he feels embarrassed because his hair has not been growing for as many years as the other priests'. As a priest, he must never cut or wash it. In a short time, it will be caked with blood, and Sonan will be proud of how he looks.

A drum begins to pound. Some prisoners from a defeated tribe are led in. No guards are needed to watch the prisoners. They will not try to escape. No matter what tribe they are from, they believe it is a privilege to die this way.

Quietly, the prisoners wait in line. One by one, they step forward. Sonan plunges his stone knife into the chest of each victim and pulls out the beating heart. Soon the steps are soaked in blood. As smoke from incense rises to the sky, Sonan and the other priests climb ladders so they can pour human blood and hearts over the giant idols in each temple. One of these is Blue Hummingbird. The idol's face and

body are covered with gold and jewels.

The bodies of the sacrifice victims will be cut into small pieces and eaten. Sonan and the other Aztecs do not eat human flesh because they are hungry. It is a religious ritual. They believe that eating the flesh of their enemies will give them great power over those tribes.

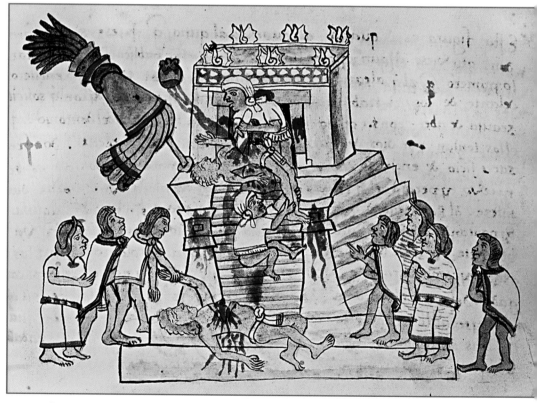

Priests sacrifice two victims to Huitzilopochtli.

THE AZTECS AND THEIR FESTIVALS

The world was a mysterious place to the Aztecs. They wondered at the movement of the moon and stars. They tried to explain the changes in weather. They feared sickness that spread through a city. But they did not know why it happened. Surely, they thought, the gods caused all these things.

Above everything, the priests told the people, the gods must be kept happy and satisfied. So the Aztecs invented festivals and rituals they believed were demanded of them.

Many of the rituals involved human sacrifices. But other events in Aztec life were more like games and sporting events.

Tlachtli (TLATCH-tlee) was an active game played by two teams. It involved a heavy rubber ball, which symbolized the sun. The players tried to hit the ball into their opponent's part of the ball court—a space about half as long as a soccer field.

Two stone rings were mounted high up on the sidewalls of the ball court. Players tried to pass the ball through one of these rings. If they succeeded, their team automatically won the game.

But this almost never happened. What made the game so

Ball court at Monte Alban

41

Tlachtli was played by the Maya and the Toltecs before the Aztecs discovered it.

difficult was that the ball could only be struck with the players' elbows, knees, or hips.

The spectators cheered and cheered. They bet heavily on which team would win. But the outcome could be even more serious. If the priests said the gods were angry that day, the men on the losing team might become human sacrifices.

In another game of skill, four men dressed as birds. They were attached to ropes by their ankles. Then they climbed to the top of a tall pole and jumped off, headfirst.

Modern volador

As a drummer pounded out a rhythm, the four men soared round and round the pole. Each man tried to fly around the pole 13 times. If they did this, the four of them would have spun for 52 circuits. This was an important number in the Aztec calendar.

No one knows what the Aztecs called this game. But when the Spaniards arrived, they named it *volador,* which in their language means "flyer."

Another, less dangerous game was patolli. This was a gambling game. Players used a board shaped like a cross. Each player had some dried beans as markers. The players sometimes gambled away all of their wealth. But at least no one could lose his life playing patolli.

How the Aztecs Kept Records

The common people of the Aztec nation could not read or write. So scribes kept records. Some kept histories. Some wrote down the laws. And others described property lines.

Whatever had to do with the gods was written by special scribes. These scribes were also priests.

When scribes wanted to write numbers, they used pictures for the numbers that all educated Aztecs recognized. These number pictures were based on 20, not 10.

The Aztecs had two calendars. One was *sacred*, or holy, and was in the form of a circle. It was divided into 13 numbers.

The other calendar was

Calendar of the sun, with the face of the sun god in the center

based on the sun. It was used by farmers and the common Aztec people. Its circle was larger than the one for the sacred calendar. The sun calendar had 20 days, which were named for things in Aztec life. Some names included Lizard, Eagle, Rabbit, or Rain. It also had five extra days. These were considered very unlucky.

Although the Aztecs used calendars in the form of a wheel, there is no evidence that they used wheeled transportation. Even though the **burdens** they carried were very heavy, the mountain roads were too steep and narrow for wheeled carts.

The two wheels turned so that each number fit with a day. So a day might be called by such a name as 1 Alligator. The days that followed would be 2 Wind, 3 House, and 4 Lizard.

Once every 52 years, the sacred and sun years began on the same day. When this happened, the Aztecs were afraid the world would end.

The Aztec scribes also made beautiful painted books called *codices*. The pages were long strips of paper made from cactus or fig leaves. These were folded like an accordion. The pages were filled with picture writing in brightly colored inks and paints. They held stories of priests and kings, pictures of Aztec life, and explanations of the movements of the stars. These picture stories took a great deal of time to produce. And only the finest painting materials were used.

AZTEC WARRIORS

Many battles were needed to enlarge the Aztec kingdom. And captured enemy soldiers were needed for sacrifice. This meant that new soldiers had to be trained each year.

Every young Aztec, except those training to be priests, was expected to fight for the kingdom. It did not matter whether his family was of the common people or the nobility.

Warrior training, like priest training, began when a young man reached the age of eight. The boys were sent to a telpochcalli. There they did lowly jobs. They scrubbed the stone steps and repaired the buildings. Late each afternoon, their teachers sent them home to help their fathers. Some worked at farming. Others learned a family craft. Then they returned to the House of Youth for the night.

When boys reached 12, they were taught to wrestle and to fight with wooden weapons. They learned the tricks of warfare. When older warriors went into battle, these young men went along to carry their supplies and help in the warrior camp.

Warrior in jaguar fur

45

From age 17 to 22, Aztec men were expected to fight in the king's army. This was a great honor. There was no pay. But no one expected any.

The special goal of each warrior was to capture three prisoners alive. As soon as a young man had done this, he was called a "master of cuts." He could show this by wearing his hair in a tuft on top of his head.

Now he was a true warrior. He could wear sandals and a loincloth. He could proudly carry a round shield with leather trim. And he would have a fine spear with a special thrower attached.

Aztec ruler Tizoc holds the hair of a conquered victim.

Two groups honored especially brave warriors. One of these was the Jaguar Knights. These men wore the fur of the jaguar into battle. The other group was the Eagle Knights. They wore helmets shaped like an eagle's head.

When time for battle came near, the bravest warriors left the city first. After a day had passed, the priests went forward in a parade. They had brilliant feathers and sacred idols strapped to their backs. Everyone believed these would aid in the victory.

On the third day, the main army began its march. These fighting men wore quilted cotton suits that had been soaked in saltwater to make the material stiff. This would make it much harder for enemies to drive spears into their bodies. These soldiers carried wooden clubs with sharp pieces of obsidian protruding from them like teeth.

The attacking Aztecs built a large bonfire to announce the beginning of the battle. As the fire rose, they tossed incense into the flames. Then the warriors danced around the bonfire. They howled, beat drums, whistled, and blew conch shells. The noise was meant to increase their excitement and to frighten their enemies.

The Aztecs did not have careful plans about how to fight an enemy. But they usually won their battles because so many of them swarmed into the foreign city. As the men in front were captured or struck down, those behind rushed forward.

As soon as the temple of the city under attack had been captured, the war was over. The victorious Aztecs sent a runner back to Tenochtitlán to announce the victory. If they lost, however, the messenger crept home and entered the city by the back gate. He wore his hair combed forward over his face to show his shame.

If an Aztec warrior died in battle or was taken prisoner and sacrificed, his family felt honored. They believed he would go to a special place called East Paradise. Here, he and the other dead warriors gathered.

The Aztec people believed that the shields and spears of their dead warriors conducted the sun to its highest point in the sky each day. And it was said that after four years, a warrior returned to Earth as a hummingbird to forever enjoy life in a garden of flowers.

Sometimes no cities were planning a war. But the Aztecs did not like peace, because without battles there would be no prisoners for sacrifices.

When they had no prisoners to offer the gods, two neighboring cities would invent a "War of the Flowers." These battles were planned like a sporting event. The two sides agreed ahead of time when and where the battle would take place and how many warriors each city would send.

The object of the War of the Flowers was to capture as many prisoners as possible. When each side was satisfied that it had enough prisoners, the armies stopped fighting and went home. With them, they took the captured men needed for their sacrificial altars.

CHAPTER 11

THE AZTECS FIND STRONG LEADERS

■ver many years, the Aztec nation grew larger and became more powerful. Finally, in 1440, a leader named Montezuma I became king. He was a fine military leader who had fought the Chalca warriors, longtime enemies of the Aztecs. He continued his military march eastward for 200 miles, until all the land from Tenochtitlán to the Gulf of Mexico was under the rule of his Aztec empire.

Montezuma I also cared about the welfare of the people in Tenochtitlán. To help them increase their farmland, he had hundreds of workers build a huge dike. It was 12 miles long. It kept back the waters of Lake Texcoco. This dike prevented flooding and allowed the farmers to reclaim the soil where the lake had once been.

Montezuma I wanted to do something about the poor water his people drank too. He ordered an **aqueduct** built to bring fresh water from the springs that ran through Chapultepec forest. The aqueduct was three miles long. It carried the pure drinking water all the way to the capital.

The Marketplace

Some of the Toltecs, who had been driven away from the valley many years before, now returned. Most were craftsmen who did fine work with both gold and feathers. Now the marketplace of Tenochtitlán was filled with handmade treasures for sale.

Each type of merchandise was assigned a special place in the marketplace. Only the finest goods made by jewelers, potters, and coppersmiths were allowed. Healers sold herbs and potions.

The Aztec nation had no official money. So people used cocoa beans for small purchases. And they bartered for more expensive goods.

To make his palace and his people even richer, Montezuma I demanded greater and greater tributes from the cities and states his warriors had conquered. The citizens of these cities were forced to send their best handwork and jewels. So many brightly colored feathers were demanded that the jungles had few birds left. In collecting these tributes, the Aztec nation grew wealthier.

The people of Spain and the rest of Europe did not know anything about this great nation in the New World. Christopher Columbus had not yet set out to sail west across the sea.

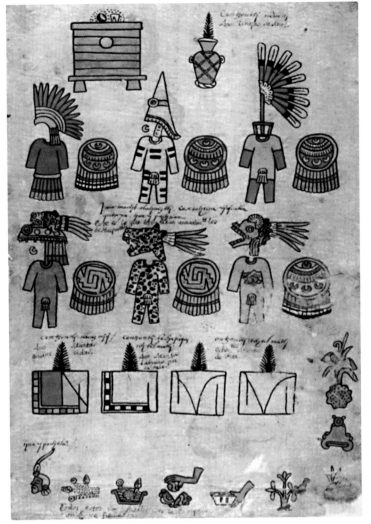

This page of the Mendosa Codex shows some of the tribute items required, including furniture, clothing, warrior costumes, and boxes of food.

Historians have found many of the Aztec codices. One of these, the Mendosa Codex, lists the tribute due each six months. About 400 towns each paid this tribute to Montezuma I.

- 2 large strings of jade beads
- 2,400 handfuls of richly colored feathers
- 160 whole bird skins
- 2 labrets of clear amber, set in gold. A labret was a type of jewelry imbedded in the lip of a noble.
- 40 jaguar skins
- 200 loaves of cocoa beans
- 800 cups of drinking cocoa
- 2 pieces of clear amber, each the size of a brick

CHAPTER 12

MONTEZUMA II BECOMES KING

After the death of Montezuma I, three other kings ruled the Aztec nation. All were from the same family.

First came Montezuma I's oldest son, Axayacatl (ash-ay-AH-katl), then his second son, Tizoc. A third son, Ahuitzotl (ah-WEET-satl), followed. All three continued to expand the kingdom.

In 1503, Ahuitzotl died in an accident. At the age of 32, his nephew Montezuma II was elected king. He was the last great leader of the Aztecs.

Although several men in his family had been a king, Montezuma II had been trained in his youth as a priest at the calmecac. So he had led a humble life. He knew how to read sacred books and chart the stars. By the time he was 18, he was both a "master of cuts" as a warrior and an honored priest.

Montezuma II

But no longer would his life be humble. No one was allowed to look at his face. If anyone dared, that person was put to death. The king was spoken to through one of his officials. When he and his chief official, the Snake Woman, were carried through the streets on litters, the common people fell to their knees.

Montezuma II moved into a huge new palace. He married many times. He took a princess from every tribe in the Aztec nation as one of his wives. His armies conquered vast new

lands, extending south to what is now Honduras. His warriors brought back not only captured craftsmen, but musicians to make life at the palace more pleasant.

Tenochtitlán became an even more glorious city. There were fine new temples, water canals, and more aqueducts to bring fresh water. Montezuma II's workers built a **causeway** across the lake wider than any ever constructed.

With Tenochtitlán at its height, the king and his chiefs controlled

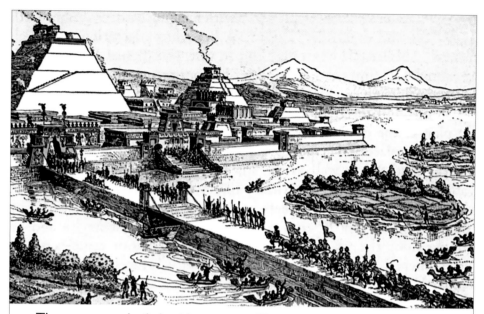

The causeway built by Montezuma II's workers was so wide that the arriving Spanish soldiers could ride their horses down it three abreast.

millions of subjects in many different cities. But these people did not feel themselves to be part of a nation. Every six months, they were forced to pay huge tributes. They longed to be rid of Montezuma II and his kingdom.

Montezuma II appointed his friends as officials. He sent merchants to spy on the people he ruled. The citizens in the captured cities paid their tribute. But they did that only because they were forced to. A few of them began to plot against the king.

Montezuma II's kingdom was large and wealthy. But it was neither happy nor secure.

And soon the Spanish would arrive in the New World. They would change Aztec life forever.

Stone standard bearer statues found at the Templo Mayor in Mexico City

As the Spaniards moved from city to city over the mountainous countryside, Cortés discovered something important and surprising about the Aztec empire.

Some tribes along his path were loyal to Montezuma II and fought fiercely to keep the Spaniards from moving westward. But in other cities, Cortés found people who hated the king's domination and the tribute they were forced to pay twice each year. These citizens, 4,000 of them, soon joined with the Spanish soldiers and sailors on the march against Tenochtitlán.

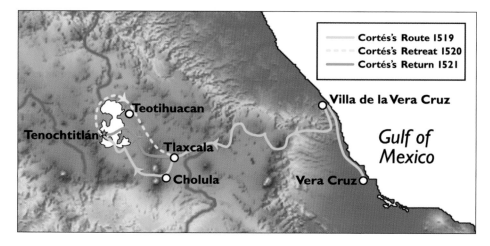

Cortés's Route 1519
Cortés's Retreat 1520
Cortés's Return 1521

Villa de la Vera Cruz

Teotihuacan

Tenochtitlán

Gulf of Mexico

Tlaxcala

Cholula

Vera Cruz

Even with the help of the Indians, Cortés did not have as many warriors as Montezuma II's vast empire did. But the Spanish had another advantage. They had weapons, such as cannons, muskets, and crossbows.

The Aztecs had seen nothing like these before. Their own simple spears and clubs would never be deadly enough to force the Spaniards back. Also, some of the Spanish men had brought huge mastiff dogs to fight by their sides.

The Aztecs were terrified. Such mysterious weapons! Such mysterious animals!

The Spanish Arrive at Tenochtitlán

When Cortés reached the outskirts of the capital, he was amazed. Tenochtitlán seemed to float before him in the distance. It was located on an island on Lake Texcoco. Passage into the city could only be made by means of one of three major causeways—from the north, south, or west.

Made of stone and rubble, these three roads were vital to the defense of the city. Just as the Spaniards were wondering how they could enter safely, the city gate opened. A procession of Aztecs in bright robes came forward to meet them.

The conquerors reached Tenochtitlán on November 8,

1519. As the Spanish troops and Indians lined up behind Cortés, Montezuma II could see that the army of fighting men stretched for miles.

He had little choice. This was not the time for a fight to the death. And he still wondered if he would be fighting the god, Quetzalcóatl.

Still unsure what to do, he greeted the Spaniards politely. Then he directed his assistants to give the newcomers a palace to stay in. For a week, there was peace between the two groups. But it was an uneasy peace.

Now another group came to see Cortés. They were the Spanish priests that had marched west with him. They demanded to know what Cortés planned to do about the Aztec temples and the sacrifices practiced there.

Wall of stone skulls uncovered at the Templo Mayor, Mexico City

The Catholic Church could not allow such brutality.

When the first week was up, Cortés looked about him. The city was crammed with Aztec warriors. Fearful that Montezuma II's men would surround and capture his army, Cortés took Montezuma II hostage and moved him into the Spanish quarters. The king, still not sure Cortés was not Quetzalcóatl, left his palace without resisting. But many of his warriors began to speak out against his peaceful ways. Each day, more of them were ready to fight the Spaniards.

The Aztecs Take Action

For many months, the Spaniards ruled the Aztecs through their prisoner-king. When Cortés left Tenochtitlán to attend to some troubles in Vera Cruz, the people of the capital rose up against the Spaniards he had left behind.

Montezuma II tried to quiet his people. Seething with anger, they threw stones at him. It is believed that one of those hurled stones struck him in the head and killed him. But some historians disagree, saying that the Spaniards murdered him.

Another leader was selected, but he soon died of smallpox brought by the invaders. He was succeeded by Cuauhtémoc (Kwow-TAY-moc). He was the 25-year-old nephew of Montezuma II.

The struggle in the city lasted for weeks. Outnumbered, the army of Hernán Cortés was finally forced to flee from Tenochtitlán. Many tried to take stolen Aztec gold with them. When the Indians surged forward and forced

them off the causeways, these foolish soldiers drowned. Instead of following the retreating Spaniards, the Aztecs stopped to recover their gold from the bodies. This allowed many of Cortés's troops to escape.

The Final Siege

The trouble at Vera Cruz that had taken Cortés away from the capital had been the arrival of another Spanish army looking for gold. When Cortés was able to defeat and kill the leader of this group, many of these new troops chose to join Cortés.

When Cortés and his men were opposed by the Indians, the soldiers killed the natives. This record shows local noblemen killed for refusing to reveal hidden treasure.

Marching from village to village, Cortés now regrouped his men and gathered more Indians to support his attacks. As he prepared for battle, Cortés now had 1,000 Spanish soldiers, 80 horses, and 75,000 Indian allies. He planned carefully for his next attack.

He ordered 13 shallow-draft boats built and then taken apart in sections. These were spirited into a hidden area near

Lake Texcoco. While he set 8,000 men to work digging a canal to the lake, others stealthily put the 13 ships back together. The preparation took many months.

During this time, Cortés enjoyed a bit of good fortune. A ship from Spain arrived at Vera Cruz loaded with new supplies of arms and gunpowder. Now he had both men and weapons. Soon he would be ready for the fight of his life.

One day at dawn, the Spaniards began launching their boats into the canal that would take them into Lake Texcoco and on to the city of Tenochtitlán. As they entered the lake, they were met by dozens of war canoes, manned by loyal Aztec warriors. But the men in the Spanish ships were armed with muskets and crossbows. The ships quickly sank the Aztec war canoes.

Now a bitter three-month battle began. Tearing down the causeways leading into Tenochtitlán, the Spaniards cut the Aztecs off from their supplies of food and fresh drinking water. No longer could the farmers reach their fields. As Cortés

Cortés and his forces overwhelm the Aztecs.

Cuauhtémoc is tortured.

advanced into the city, his men tore down buildings and filled the canals with the rubble.

As weeks went by, the Aztecs were weakened by hunger, thirst, and illnesses—smallpox and measles—that had been brought to the New World by the Spaniards.

Many Aztecs were dead. The rest were sick or starving. They had lost their will to fight.

Cuauhtémoc and his family tried to flee in a canoe. But they were chased down by one of the Spanish ships and brought before Cortés. Cuauhtémoc was taken to a prison and later put to death.

On August 13, 1521, after 75 days of fighting, the Aztec capital and its weary defenders fell.

The Aztecs were allowed to govern themselves for a short time. But they were forced to end their human sacrifices.

After a short time, the greed of the Spanish conquerors took over. The defeated Aztecs were brought together, branded, and forced to work in the gold and silver mines. Many became slaves on the great farms of the conquerors.

A stern ruler, Cortés governed his adopted land until 1534 when King Charles appointed another royal governor. Relieved of his command, Cortés returned to Spain for a long-awaited visit with his family. His visit complete, he prepared to return to the New World. But he fell ill and died at the port of Seville before he could even board his ship.

Sure it would be his wish, his family ordered Cortés's body carried across the sea and buried in Mexico.

THE AZTECS OF TODAY

Even though the Spaniards of the 1500s brought Aztec rule to an end, they did not destroy the native culture. And they did not fully destroy the capital, Tenochtitlán. The modern-day capital, Mexico City, is located on the same site in the Valley of Mexico.

Nahuatl, the Aztec language, is still spoken in Mexico by some 5,000 citizens. And now most Mexicans belong to the Roman Catholic Church. But some traditions of the Aztec religion remain. Paper flowers still decorate the tombs of the dead, just as real flowers once did. Skull-shaped candies, so popular with children, are a tradition that comes from the days of the Aztec priests and the masks they wore.

If you visit Mexico today, you will see women in beautiful embroidered blouses with designs like those worn by the Aztec nobility. Dance troupes perform the ceremonial dances of their ancestors. Museums are filled with objects from the past. And if you attend a festival, you may be lucky enough to see voladors, dressed in bird costumes, spinning by their ankles from a center pole far above your head.

GLOSSARY

aqueduct	structure for carrying a large quantity of water
artisan	craftsman
barbarian	land, culture, or people thought to be inferior to another land, culture, or people
barter	to exchange one good for another
burden	something that is carried; load
canal	artificial waterway
causeway	raised road across wet ground or water
conch	spiral-shaped shell
dike	bank of earth used to control water flow
eclipse	total or partial blocking of one celestial (of outer space) body by another
embroidered	having decorative hand-sewn stitches
fast	to not eat food
ferment	to change into alcohol
hillock	small mound
humility	quality of not being proud
loincloth	garment worn around the hips in warmer climates
meter	unit of measure equal to about 39.37 inches
obsidian	dark natural glass
reclaim	to rescue from an undesirable state
scribe	copier or writer of records
thatch	plant material used to cover a shelter
tribute	payment by one nation or ruler to another

INDEX

This chacmool from the Templo Mayor shrine to Tlaloc held the hearts and blood of people sacrificed. It has been dated to around 1390 A.D.